# Literary Newsmakers for Students, Volume 2

**Project Editor**
Anne Marie Hacht **Editorial**
Ira Mark Milne

**Rights Acquisition and Management**
Margaret Chamberlain-Gaston and Robyn Young
**Manufacturing**
Rita Wimberly

**Imaging**
Lezlie Light, Mike Logusz, and Kelly Quin
**Product Design**
Pamela A. E. Galbreath **Vendor Administration**
Civie Green **Product Manager**
Meggin Condino © 2006 Gale, a part of Cengage Learning Inc.

Cengage and Burst Logo are trademarks and Gale is a registered trademark used herein under license.

*For more information, contact*
Gale, an imprint of Cengage Learning

27500 Drake Rd.
Farmington Hills, MI 48331-3535
Or you can visit our Internet site at http://www.gale.com **ALL RIGHTS RESERVED**
No part of this work covered by the copyright hereon may be reproduced or used in any form or by any means—graphic, electronic, or mechanical, including photocopying, recording, taping, Web distribution, or information storage retrieval systems—without the written permission of the publisher.

For permission to use material from this product, submit your request via Web at http://www.gale-edit.com/permissions, or you may download our Permissions Request form and submit your request by fax or mail to: *Permissions Department*
Gale, an imprint of Cengage Learning
27500 Drake Rd.
Farmington Hills, MI 48331-3535
Permissions Hotline:
248-699-8006 or 800-877-4253, ext. 8006
Fax: 248-699-8074 or 800-762-4058

Since this page cannot legibly accommodate all copyright notices, the acknowledgments constitute an extension of the copyright notice.

While every effort has been made to ensure the reliability of the information presented in this publication, Gale, an imprint of Cengage Learning does not guarantee the accuracy of the data contained herein. Gale, an imprint of Cengage Learning accepts no payment for listing; and inclusion in the publication of any organization, agency, institution, publication, service, or individual does not imply endorsement of the editors or publisher. Errors brought to the attention of the publisher and verified to the satisfaction of the publisher will be corrected in future editions.

**ISBN 13:** 978-1-4144-0282-6
**ISBN 10:** 1-4144-0282-1
ISSN: 1559-9639

This title is also available as an e-book
ISBN-13: 978-1-4144-2930-4, ISBN-10: 1-4144-2930-4
Contact your Gale, an imprint of Cengage Learning representative for ordering information.

Printed in the United States of America

10 9 8 7 6 5 4 3 2 1

# *Vernon God Little*

**DBC Pierre**

**2003**

## Introduction

In *Vernon God Little*, first-time author DBC Pierre dares to go where many would not. The book is an absurdly humorous look at the misadventures of a Texas teen named Vernon Little whose best friend in the world has just killed sixteen of their classmates and himself. In the wake of the tragedy, the townspeople seek both answers and vengeance; because Vernon was the killer's closest friend, he becomes the focus of their fury.

The book tackles many aspects of modern American society, including mindless consumer culture, the death penalty for minors, news reporters casting tragedy as entertainment, and average citizens who crave fame. The book is narrated by Vernon, described by Sam Sifton of the *New York Times Book Review* as "a deceptively simple boy who narrates this tale in the manner of a character created by Mark Twain and remixed by Dr. Dre." The book's unique narrative style has drawn comparisons to both J. D. Salinger's *The Catcher in the Rye* and Mark Twain's *The Adventures of Huckleberry Finn*.

The novel, published in the United States by Harvest Books, has proven especially successful in Great Britain, where it was first published. Some critics have suggested that its scathing negative portrayal of American society is too off-putting for readers in the United States, where it has been less successful; others have suggested that its over-the-top absurdity is a frighteningly accurate assessment of how foreigners view the United States and its citizens. In any case, *Vernon God Little* has been awarded both the 2003 Man Booker Prize and the 2003 Whitbread Award for Best First Novel, and it remains one of only a handful of high-profile literary works to tackle the subject of school shootings in America.

## Author Biography

DBC Pierre is the pseudonym for author Peter Finley, who was born in Australia in 1961. (The author has reported that the "DBC" stands for "Dirty But Clean.") Pierre grew up in Mexico City, but he spent significant time living in Texas as well. In an interview with the *Guardian* (U.K.), Pierre explains his varied upbringing:

> I grew up with a real sense of cultural homelessness.... I haven't been successful in fitting in anywhere. I clearly wasn't Mexican, although I could move in that culture as easily as anywhere. I'm a British national but wasn't quite from here; and I went to school with a lot of expat Americans.... There's nothing I love more than to just be part of something, for someone to pay you a hello.

After his father died of a brain tumor when Pierre was nineteen, Pierre—as the default male head of his household—began to accrue both mounting debts and an increasingly destructive cocaine habit. He spent the following decade recovering from both, and he eventually found a job as a graphic designer. In 2000, Pierre moved to Ireland where, in an attempt to finally recover from his debts, he undertook what he calls "a big and bold stroke"—the writing of his first novel, *Vernon God Little*.

*Vernon God Little* was published by Faber and Faber in 2003 and went on to win several distinguished literary awards, including the Man Booker Prize, the Whitbread First Novel Award, and the Bollinger Everyman Wodehouse Prize. The novel was also listed as a *New York Times* Notable Book of 2003. Pierre published a follow-up novel, *Ludmila's Broken English*, in 2006. In a statement posted on the British website Contemporary Writers, Pierre reveals, "I write because it is the most bright and intimate relationship I will ever have with other minds." As of 2006, Pierre lives in Ireland and continues to write fiction.

# Plot Summary

## *Act I: S—t Happened*

### Chapters 1-6

*Vernon God Little* is narrated by Vernon Gregory Little, an outcast fifteen-year-old in the small Texas town of Martirio. The book opens on a Friday—three days after one of Vernon's friends, Jesus, went on a shooting spree at the local high school before killing himself.

Vernon is brought in to the police station for questioning about the shooting; as he describes it, "I sit waiting between shafts of light from a row of doorways, naked except for my shoes and Thursday's underwear." Deputy Vaine Gurie enters; she gives him back his clothes and asks him what he knows about the shootings. The Guries are a large, prominent family in town. Vernon tells her he does not know anything—in fact, he was not even in class when it happened. Gurie, knowing Vernon was a close friend of Jesus, does not believe him. Sheriff Porkorney does not seem to believe Vernon either, and he suggests that he might have been Jesus's gay lover.

Vernon's mother, Doris, sends her best friend, Palmyra—known as Pam—to the police station to pick up Vernon and bring him home, because Doris is waiting for her new side-by-side refrigerator to be delivered. According to Vernon, Pam is "fatter than Mom, so Mom feels good around her. Mom's other friends are slimmer. They're not her best friends." Pam collects Vernon and whisks him away without waiting for permission from the police.

Back at the Little residence, Doris, Pam, and Vernon find Gurie waiting. She accuses him of fleeing from his interview, and just as she prepares to take him back to the station, Doris's gossipy friends—Leona Dunt, Georgette Porkorney, and Betty Pritchard, as well as Betty's ten-year-old son Brad—pull up to the house. In the midst of the commotion, a reporter named Eulalio Ledesma approaches Gurie with a camera and begins to interview her. Ledesma scares Gurie away with his questions, and the reporter tells Vernon that he owes him a story for the favor.

Doris asks Vernon to invite Ledesma inside the house for a drink, and he accepts. On the way to the house, Ledesma tells Vernon that he needs to tell his story to the world to show his innocence. Inside the house, Ledesma, who prefers to go by the nickname Lally, tells the gathering of women that drug-sniffing dogs are being brought in to investigate a drug connection to the shootings. Hearing this, Vernon secretly pockets some marijuana and LSD from his closet. Though the drugs belong to an older girl named Taylor Figueroa who is away at college, Vernon decides he must ditch them to protect himself. The next morning, after getting his hair cut, Vernon accidentally reveals the marijuana to Lally during the drive home in Lally's van. Lally takes the marijuana and stashes it in his seat. Vernon dissolves the LSD in a ginseng energy drink and hides it in his room. Soon after, Vaine Gurie arrives to arrest Vernon; she tells him that they found his fingerprints at the scene of the crime. As he is taken away, Vernon asks Lally to tell the world the truth about his innocence.

In jail, Vernon imagines that he will escape to Mexico and live in a beach house with the girl of his dreams, Taylor Figueroa. Several years older than Vernon, she is attending college in Houston. Vernon recalls with some regret how he helped a drunken Taylor into a car one night before she graduated, and though he had an opportunity to take advantage of her, he instead located one of her friends to watch over her.

The next day, Vernon meets his court-appointed lawyer, Mr. Abdini. While on recess during his first court proceeding, he sees Lally's news story about him. Lally has betrayed him and deliberately makes Vernon look guilty. Back in court, the judge orders Vernon to undergo a psychiatric evaluation. Vernon sits in jail awaiting his evaluation, nervous because the police are looking for a second weapon to tie him to the crime, and he knows his father's gun—covered with his fingerprints—is out there, just waiting to be found.

## *Act II: How I Spent My Summer Vacation*

## Chapters 7-13

Vernon is taken to see Dr. Oliver Goosens, the same psychiatrist who had treated Jesus before he went on his rampage. Vernon opens up and explains his situation to the doctor:

> See, first everybody dissed me because my buddy was Mexican, then because he was weird, but I stood by him, I thought friendship was a sacred thing—then it all went to hell, and now I'm being punished for it, they're twisting every regular little fact to fit my guilt.

Vernon tells Goosens his alibi for the shootings: He was away from school on an errand and stopped to use the bathroom—a slave to his unpredictable bowels. Goosens then asks Vernon to undress, and he begins to touch Vernon inappropriately. Vernon leaps up in protest, and as he leaves, Goosens threatens to file an unfavorable report about his mental state. Back in jail, Vernon notes: "I sense a learning: that much dumber people than you end up in charge." At his bail proceeding, the judge sets Vernon free without bail, but he orders him to submit to treatment by Goosens or else he will return to jail. The judge also suggests that Vernon and his lawyer try to confirm his alibi. Vernon is not about to do that, because he happened to defecate right next to a gun covered with his fingerprints.

Back home, Vernon finds that Lally has

infiltrated his house and has begun an affair with his mother, Doris. Unwilling to return to Goosens, Vernon decides to enact his plan to flee to Mexico. He walks to the Greyhound bus station, but just before he can buy a ticket, Pam shows up and drags him back home.

The next day, the community holds a Tragedy Sale to display its spirit in the wake of the shootings. Vernon is forced to work one of the booths wearing a choir gown. While at the booth, Vernon learns that a posse is being formed to search for the second weapon, and that they will be searching near Keeter's property—which is where the gun with his prints is located. Vernon offers to pay a boy to watch his booth for an hour, though he does not plan on returning. He plans to find the gun, wipe off his prints, and head to Mexico until things cool down. On the way, he is stopped by one of Lally's old associates, and he learns that Lally is not really a reporter from CNN as he has claimed but is simply a television repairman from Nacogdoches looking for his shot at fame.

Vernon rides out to Keeter's, or as he calls it, "The edge of the universe of town." It is a barren expanse of land with a junkyard and an old mine shaft, which Vernon calls the den; this is where the second weapon—and his DNA from that fateful day—are hidden. On the way there, Vernon is stopped by Tyrie Lasseen, the man who runs the junkyard. Lasseen tells Vernon to leave the area, and Vernon is soon spotted by both Ella Bouchard, a tactless girl who has a crush on him, as well as the search party looking for the gun. He rides off, heading home to grab some items to sell or pawn for his escape.

Vernon finds himself trapped at home with his mother and her friends. Lally's true identity is revealed when his disabled mother calls the Little house, though no one believes it except for Vernon. Lally decides to move in with Leona to keep his past at bay, which breaks Doris's heart. Early the next morning, while Doris is away visiting Vernon's grandmother, Vernon gathers some items to pawn and leaves the house. Instead of fleeing, he gets drunk and high, and then he returns home later in the day to check on his mother.

Back at home, Vernon promises his mother that he will somehow get sixty dollars to keep their power from being shut off. He also catches a glimpse of a news story from California about another school shooting. Vernon decides what he must do: "I have to learn how to turn slime into legitimate business, the way it's my right to do in this free world." He picks up Ella and takes her to the home of Mr. Deutschman, a former school principal who is rumored to lust after young girls. Ella agrees to seduce Mr. Deutschman so Vernon can take an incriminating photo and extort some cash from the man. The two end up getting only $140 to split between them; Ella agrees to give sixty dollars to Vernon's mother so she can pay the electric bill. Then she gives Vernon her share of the money and kisses him on the cheek, professing her love for him before she disappears. With Lally and Vaine after him with a SWAT team, Vernon escapes into the night.

## *Act III: Against All Odds*

### *Chapters 14-18*

A few miles outside of Martirio, Vernon flags down a bus bound for San Antonio and convinces the driver to let him board. In San Antonio, Vernon gets Taylor Figueroa's phone number in Houston and calls her. At first she does not remember him, and when she does, she still seems uninterested; after Vernon reveals that he is on the run from the law, however, Taylor agrees to meet him at a mall in Houston later that afternoon. "See how things work?" Vernon asks the reader. "First I'm like a skidmark on her mouthpiece, and she wants to wind up the call. But see what happens now I'm in *trouble*. See the awesome power of *trouble*."

Vernon buys a ticket to Houston, and when he arrives, he sells some of his things at a pawn shop to add to his bankroll. He meets Taylor at the mall. As they drink juice together, Taylor reveals her desire to be on television, as well as her relationship with an older, wealthy man. The conversation is interrupted when Leona, who happens to be Taylor's cousin, shows up. Vernon flees before he can be spotted and takes a bus to McAllen, a town on the Texas-Mexico border. On a television in the bus station, he learns that Officer Barry Gurie has been killed in Martitio, and that Lally is touting a connection between that incident and the school shootings.

Vernon walks to the bridge that marks the border between the United States and Mexico. He is pulled aside by a Mexican police officer who asks to see his identification. Vernon has none, and at first the officer refuses to let him enter Mexico; however, a twenty-dollar bribe helps change the officer's mind. He makes his way on foot toward Monterrey, stopping in a bar the following night. He has no money, but he trades some music CDs for alcohol, and drinks all night long.

He wakes in the morning to find that he has traded away his clothes and shoes for shabby replacements and a couple hundred pesos. A newfound friend from the bar, a truck driver named Pelayo, agrees to take Vernon to his home in Guerrero. Pelayo, his ten-year-old son, and Vernon ride across Mexico together, eventually reaching Acapulco, where Pelayo must drop off cargo before returning to Guerrero. Vernon calls Taylor from Acapulco and asks her to send him money, and she agrees to wire him six hundred dollars, though it will not arrive for two days. In the meantime, Vernon goes to Guerrero where Pelayo takes him to a beach house straight out of his dreams and tells Vernon he can stay there for a couple of days, or longer if he wishes.

Vernon returns to Acapulco two days later. It is Monday, and it is Vernon's sixteenth birthday. He approaches the Western Union counter, but instead of a wire transfer, Vernon finds Taylor Figueroa waiting for him in person with the cash. Taylor takes Vernon to a hotel room and seduces him. As she does, she asks Vernon to tell her that he killed for her; in the heat of the moment, Vernon says what she wants to hear. Immediately, the seduction comes to a halt and officers storm the room to arrest Vernon. He is flown to Houston, where he receives a new lawyer who looks like actor Brian Dennehy. There, far from Martirio, he will be put on trial for murder.

## *Act IV: How My Summer Vacation Spent Me*

### *Chapters 19-22*

Vernon is tried not only for the sixteen murders at his high school, but for even more murders around the state for which suggestible witnesses identify him as the killer. Vernon's lawyer does an admirable job of refuting the prosecutor's claims that Vernon went on a rampage throughout the state after the school shootings. He also exposes Oliver Goosens as a pedophile who runs a child pornography website and discredits Taylor Figueroa as a girl who not only paid Vernon for sex, but flew to Mexico under the direction of Lally in an attempt to entrap Vernon. The lawyer's efforts to expose Lally are less successful, and when Vernon is tricked into testifying, the prosecutor manages to make Vernon look guilty despite his innocence.

Vernon flashes back to the day of the shootings. He is in Mr. Nuckles's science class with Jesus; a bully named Max Lechuga relentlessly taunts Jesus, implying that he is gay. Other students join in, and Nuckles does little to stop the harassment. Just as Max moves to show the class naked pictures of Jesus—presumably taken by Oliver Goosens—Jesus runs away. Lori Donner, Jesus's only other friend besides Vernon, chases after him. Nuckles gives Vernon some handwritten notes and asks him to take the notes to the lab and find a candle for a class experiment.

Lori tells Vernon that Jesus has fled on his bike, and Vernon rides off in pursuit. Vernon goes to the den at the old mine shaft on Keeter's property, but he finds that Jesus has already been there. Jesus's gun is missing from the locked box where it usually rests, and he is already on his way back to the school. Vernon is suddenly overcome by a need to defecate, which he does, using Nuckles's science notes as toilet paper.

By the time Vernon gets back to school, sixteen students have already been killed. Vernon finds Jesus's gym bag, still half-filled with ammunition, and learns from a wounded Mr. Nuckles that Jesus has accidentally shot Lori, his only other friend, during the rampage. Vernon sees Jesus over her body, anguished at his mistake. Vernon turns away just as Jesus takes his own life. Mr. Nuckles recoils as Vernon tries to help him, and Vernon realizes that, because he still holds Jesus's gym bag, Nuckles thinks Vernon is an accessory to the murders.

Nuckles shows up in court to testify against Vernon, and the young man's fate is sealed. Though he is cleared of the murders that took place after the school shootings, Vernon is found guilty of murdering sixteen of his fellow students.

## *Act V: Me Ves y Sufres*

### *Chapters 23-27*

Vernon is on death row awaiting execution by Christmas, even though he is not yet old enough to vote. Lally continues to expand his media empire, and he manages to turn death row into a reality television event where viewers can vote for who they would like to see executed next. While on death row, Vernon is taken to meet a man known as Pastor Lasalle, who tells Vernon not to rely on a higher power to make things right: "You're the God. Take responsibility. Exercise your power." Vernon then discovers that Lasalle is actually another death-row convict, and that he has been chosen by home viewers as the first to be executed under the new system.

Vernon lasts through several more execution votes, but eventually he is chosen as the next to go. On March 28, the day he is scheduled to die, Vernon reveals to Lally the location of his gun as well as the key to the lock that protects it. He also gives information to Vaine Gurie and Taylor Figueroa, setting his secret plan into motion.

For his final meal, Vernon gets a *Chik'n'Mix Choice Supreme* from the *Bar-B-Chew Barn*. For his final song, he requests "Galveston" by Glen

Campbell. As he enters the room where he will receive his lethal injection, Vernon takes off his shirt to reveal a homemade tattoo across his chest: *"Me ves y sufres,"* or "See me and suffer." In the witness area, Vernon sees Mrs. Speltz, the mother of one of the shooting victims, and Ella Bouchard, who has grown into a lovely young woman. Vernon feels the needle in his arm, and drifts off into a dream.

In his dream, he sees Lally get the padlock key from Vernon's room, as well as the bottle of LSD-laced energy drink that Vernon had stashed with it long before. Georgette and Betty follow Lally as he makes his way to Keeter's; he drinks the drug-laced energy drink on the way there. Lally discovers the second weapon at the mine shaft and begins hallucinating from the drugs in his system. Vaine Gurie and Taylor Figueroa arrive on the scene, and when Lally points the weapon at Taylor, Vaine and her team open fire on Lally. Georgette and Betty arrive on the scene to search for Vernon's feces, but they find that it is already gone.

Vernon wakes from his dream to find that he is still alive. As he waits for the killing solution to enter his veins, his former lawyer, Mr. Abdini, bursts into the witness area holding a melted candle and Mr. Nuckles's science notes that Vernon used as toilet paper on the day of the shooting. Vernon's pardon comes through at the last possible moment.

Vernon is freed from jail, and his mother, Doris, finally receives the side-by-side refrigerator she has been waiting for. Vernon's dried feces makes the cover of *Time* magazine, and a note Jesus left with the second weapon suggests that both Goosens and Nuckles had sexually abused him. Justice will finally prevail. Vernon prepares to head to Mexico with Ella, and as he tells an elderly neighbor before they leave, "Everything's back to normal."

# Characters

## *Abdini*

Mr. Abdini is Vernon's original lawyer as appointed by the court in Martirio. Although his is portrayed as rather incompetent, Abdini is the person who vows to prove Vernon's alibi. While Vernon is on the gurney awaiting death, Abdini bursts into the witness area holding Marion Nuckles's lab notes, which Vernon used to wipe himself after defecating out at Keeter's at the time of the shootings.

*↳ his comedic element makes him seem incompentent*

## *Ella Bouchard*

Ella Bouchard is a younger classmate of Vernon who has a crush on him. According to Vernon, "Ella's just skinny, with some freckles, and this big ole head of tangly blond hair that's always blown to hell, like a Barbie doll your dog's been chewing on for a month." Ella helps Vernon earn some money for his escape through questionable means, and when he eventually gets out of jail, Ella —who has grown into a beautiful young woman— is waiting for him.

## Media Adaptations

- An abridged audio recording of *Vernon God Little* was released by Penguin Audiobooks in 2004. The book is read by Ewen Bremner and is currently available on compact disc or as an audio download through www.audible.com.

## *Brian Dennehy*

Brian Dennehy is the name Vernon gives to his lawyer in Houston who represents him during his murder trial. Vernon compares the lawyer to the movie star Brian Dennehy, and describes him as "all burly and wise.... I'm damn hopeful, and I just know the jury will love him, they'll be wishing he was their dad, all crusty and benign."

## *Deutschman*

Mr. Deutschman is a former school principal who lives in a poor section of Martirio. He is rumored to enjoy the company of young girls, and Ella Bouchard tells Vernon that Deutschman once gave her a Coke in exchange for allowing him to touch her bottom. When Vernon is desperate for money, he and Ella go to Mr. Deutschman's house; Ella lures Mr. Deutschman into a compromising position, and then Vernon photographs the two of them. He extorts $140 from Mr. Deutschman in exchange for the picture.

## *Leona Dunt*

Leona Dunt is one of Doris Little's group of friends. She, Georgette Porkorney, and Betty Pritchard regularly visit Doris in Leona's Eldorado, possessing an uncanny ability to show up just as things get interesting. According to Vernon, Leona is "an almost pretty blonde with a honeysuckle voice you know got its polish from rubbing on her last husband's wallet." Leona always feels the need to upstage her friends by bragging about things she has bought or trips she has planned. When Lally decides he must move out of the Little house, Leona takes him in and believes he will help her become an anchorwoman for CNN. Leona is also Taylor Figueroa's cousin, and she shows up in Houston while Vernon meets with Taylor.

## *Eileena*

Eileena is the receptionist at the Martirio police station. When Vernon is being held for questioning, Palmyra sweet-talks Eileena into letting her take Vernon home against Vaine Gurie's orders.

## *Taylor Figueroa*

Taylor Figueroa is a former student at the Martirio high school who has gone on to attend college in Houston. When she was a senior, Vernon helped take care of her one night after she got drunk at a party. Afterward, he regrets that he missed his opportunity to take advantage of her. When he decides to escape to Mexico, the only girl he considers taking with him is Taylor.

When Vernon actually does run away from Martirio, he calls Taylor to try and get her to go to Mexico with him. He meets her in Houston, but he must flee before he has a chance to ask her. After Vernon arrives in Acapulco, he calls Taylor and asks her for some money; she surprises him by showing up in Acapulco in person. Taylor then seduces Vernon in an attempt to extract a murder confession from him. It is later revealed in court that Taylor's trip to Mexico was financed by Lally.

In Vernon's dream while on the execution gurney, Taylor shows up at Keeter's after Lally has found the second gun. Lally, hallucinating because of the LSD in his system, mistakes Taylor for his mother and shoots at her before he is killed by police. Although Vernon never specifies how Taylor is injured during the incident, in the last chapter he states, "She'll be fine. Just maybe not filling out her panties the way she used to."

## *Oliver Goosens*

Doctor Oliver Goosens is the psychiatrist assigned by the court to evaluate Vernon's mental well-being. He attempts to sexually assault Vernon during his examination, and he threatens to write a negative report about Vernon if he resists. Vernon flees, and Goosens later testifies that Vernon exhibits classic psychopathic tendencies.

During Vernon's murder trial, Vernon's lawyer exposes Goosens as a pedophile who operates a child pornography website called *Serenade of Sodom*. Later, Jesus's final letter suggests that Goosens, like Nuckles, had been sexually assaulting Jesus in the days and weeks leading up to the shootings.

## *Gregson*

Mr. Gregson is the prosecutor who argues against Vernon being freed on bail after he is first arrested. It is Gregson who suggests in court that there may be a second weapon involved in the murders at the high school.

## *Barry Gurie*

Barry Gurie is a detention officer at the Martirio police station, and the husband of Vaine Gurie. Barry watches over Vernon when he is first arrested, and he frequently taunts the boy for his own amusement. According to Doris's gossipy friends, Barry has threatened to leave Vaine if she does not lose weight within a month. Barry is killed while on a SWAT raid looking for Vernon. Vernon is tried for, but acquitted of, murdering him.

## *Helen Gurie*

Judge Helen Gurie is the judge who presides over Vernon's bail proceedings after he is first arrested. Although Judge Gurie at first appears sympathetic to Vernon's situation, her opinion seems to change when she learns of Vernon's less wholesome side. Still, Judge Gurie allows Vernon to be released without bail, provided he agrees to meet regularly with Doctor Goosens.

## *Vaine Gurie*

Deputy Vaine Gurie is an officer for the Martirio Police Department. She is the primary police officer dealing with Vernon and his possible involvement in the school shooting. Although she tells people that she is on a diet, Vaine eats things like barbecued ribs when none of her friends can see. She is married to Barry Gurie, the detention officer for Martirio's tiny jail.

## *Jones*

Officer Jones is the guard who watches over the inmates on death row. Jones appears to treat Vernon and the other prisoners well, though he sometimes tells Vernon that his pardon came through just for laughs.

## *Lasalle*

Lasalle is a convict on death row with Vernon. The other convicts treat him as a holy man and refer to him as "Pastor Lasalle." Vernon is allowed to visit Lasalle twice during his stay on death row. The second visit takes place shortly before Lasalle is executed. Lasalle offers Vernon this advice: "Don't be lookin up at no sky for help. Look down here, at us twisted dreamers.... You're the God. Take responsibility. Exercise your power." Vernon later learns that Lasalle is the same axe-murderer he saw on television the year before, dozing in the same hall of the Martirio police station where Vernon sits at the start of the novel.

## *Tyrie Lasseen*

Tyrie Lasseen is the man in charge of the junkyard found on Keeter's property at the edge of Martirio. When Vernon rides out to Keeter's to try and get his father's gun before the search party finds it, Lasseen disrupts Vernon's plan and tells him to clear out of the area.

## *Max Lechuga*

Max Lechuga is one of the sixteen students Jesus shoots down at the high school. Max is the main student who taunts Jesus in Mr. Nuckles's science class on the day of the shooting. He even puts nude pictures of Jesus on the screen savers of the computer terminals in the classroom.

## *Nancie Lechuga*

Nancie Lechuga is Max Lechuga's mother. After her son is killed in the school shooting, she appears to have a breakdown. At the start of the novel, Vernon indicates that she stood all night in the middle of the road after hearing the news; afterward, her presence is identified only by a movement of drapes in the front window of her house. Nancie Lechuga is the former leader of Doris Little's group of friends.

## *Eulalio Ledesma*

Eulalio Ledesma, also known as Lally, is a television repairman from Nacogdoches who comes to Martirio and pretends to be a CNN correspondent. He insinuates himself into the Little household, and he creates a news story that portrays Vernon as a knowing accomplice to the murders. Thanks to the exclusive information he obtains about Vernon, Lally ultimately succeeds in becoming a media star, even creating a new reality television show where viewers can choose which death row inmate should be the next prisoner executed.

In Vernon's dream while on the execution gurney, Lally drinks the LSD-laced energy drink Vernon has hidden in his room; he then drives to Keeter's and retrieves the second weapon, but begins to have hallucinations. He is shot by Vaine Gurie's team of officers when he points Vernon's father's gun at Taylor Figueroa.

## *Lally Ledesma*

*See* Eulalio Ledesma.

## *Doris Little*

Vernon's mother, Doris, is an overweight widow who takes in unscrupulous reporter Eulalio Ledesma despite the protests of her son. She has an affair with Ledesma, who ultimately betrays both Vernon and Doris in his quest for fame. Doris is portrayed as selfish, melodramatic, and gullible throughout the book, and she seems more concerned with getting a new refrigerator than with helping her son prove his innocence. Toward the end of the novel, the author hints that Doris may have actually played a role in the disappearance of her first husband, and that he might be buried in the yard beneath her decorative bench.

## *Vernon Gregory Little*

Vernon Little is a fifteen-year-old boy who lives in the central Texas town of Martirio. Vernon is an outcast, with a missing father and a mother who seems to care more about a new side-by-side refrigerator than about her son's welfare. Vernon's life is greatly complicated when his closest friend, Jesus Navarro, shoots sixteen of their fellow high school students before turning the gun on himself. Suspected of being an accomplice to the murders, Vernon is portrayed in the media as a deviant and a psychopath, and he is convicted despite a complete lack of evidence against him.

## *Jesus Navarro*

Jesus Navarro is Vernon's former best friend, and the boy who shoots sixteen of his fellow students at the high school before taking his own life. Before the shootings, Vernon notes that Jesus "keeps secrets from me, like he never did before. He got weird. Nobody knows why." After the shootings, the reason for Jesus's change in behavior eventually becomes clear. At the time of his death, Jesus was wearing a pair of silk panties bought for him by Doctor Goosens. Later, a letter left by Jesus indicates that both Mr. Nuckles and Doctor Goosens had been sexually abusing him.

## *Marion Nuckles*

Marion Nuckles is a science teacher at the Martirio high school. It is during his class that Jesus flees and returns to school with his gun. Nuckles is the only survivor of the shooting who can confirm Vernon's alibi, since he sent Vernon to retrieve a candle before the shootings; however, when Nuckles later sees Vernon holding Jesus's gym bag full of ammunition, he becomes convinced that Vernon is an accomplice to the murders.

Vernon mentions that Nuckles spent a great deal of time with Jesus before the shootings, and he even recommended that Jesus visit Doctor Goosens. Eventually, authorities discover a note from Jesus that suggests both Nuckles and Goosens had been sexually abusing Jesus.

## *Palmyra*

Palmyra, also known as Pam, is Doris Little's best friend. Since Doris does not have a car, Palmyra frequently transports Vernon around town. Palmyra is more overweight than Doris, and throughout the novel her main concern seems to be whether or not Vernon is eating regularly. Palmyra's Mercury has a cassette of *The Best of Glen Campbell* stuck in its stereo, so that is the only music she listens to while driving.

## *Pelayo*

Pelayo is the Mexican truck driver whom Vernon meets at a bar while walking toward Monterrey. After a night of drinking together, Pelayo—who is also traveling with his ten-year-old son—agrees to take Vernon back to his home town of Guerrero. Pelayo arranges for Vernon to stay for free at a small beach house in Guerrero, just like in Vernon's fantasy. On the back of Pelayo's truck are printed the words, "*Me ves, y sufres*," which means "See me, and suffer." Vernon later tattoos these words across his chest prior to his scheduled execution.

## *Georgette Porkorney*

Georgette is one of Doris Little's friends. Vernon describes her as "a dry ole buzzard with hair of lacquered tobacco smoke." She is always accompanied by Betty Pritchard, and she is usually found smoking a cigarette. Georgette is married to Sheriff Porkorney. In Vernon's dream while on the execution gurney, Georgette and Betty search the den at Keeter's in search of Vernon's feces.

## *Porkorney*

Sheriff Porkorney is the leader of Martirio's police force. At the beginning of the novel, Sheriff Porkorney questions Vernon regarding his whereabouts during the shootings. Porkorney also suggests that Vernon is Jesus Navarro's gay lover. Sheriff Porkorney is married to Georgette Porkorney, one of Doris Little's group of friends.

## *Betty Pritchard*

Betty Pritchard is one of Doris Little's group of friends. She seems permanently attached to

Georgette Porkorney; as Vernon puts it, "Betty just has this mopey face, and tags along saying, 'I know, I *know*.'" Betty has a ten-year-old son named Brad whom she often brings to the Little house.

## *Brad Pritchard*

Brad Pritchard is Betty Pritchard's ten-year-old son. Vernon reveals that Brad once broke his PlayStation, but he was never punished because he reportedly has some kind of unspecified disorder "that works like a Get Out of Jail Free card." Brad often antagonizes Vernon throughout the novel.

## *Lorna Speltz*

Lorna Speltz is one of the students killed by Jesus Navarro in the shooting at the Martirio high school. On the morning of the shootings, she participates in the taunting of Jesus during Nuckles's science class. Vernon describes Lorna as "a girl who's on a time-delay from the rest of us."

## *Speltz*

Mrs. Speltz is the mother of Lorna Speltz, one of the students killed in the high school shootings. She appears at Vernon's preliminary hearing in Martirio, and she later shows up as a witness to Vernon's execution.

# Themes

## *Tragedy and Entertainment*

The story of *Vernon God Little* begins after a devastating tragedy: Just three days earlier, Vernon's friend Jesus Navarro gunned down sixteen of his classmates and then killed himself. All of the events in the novel are spawned by this single tragic event. In addition, Vernon's experiences amount to a secondary tragedy in the wake of the shootings: He is unfairly accused of being an accomplice to the murders; the only people he cares about seem to care less about him than about fame and worldly goods; and he is sentenced to death despite his innocence and a complete lack of evidence against him.

The tragedy depicted in *Vernon God Little*, however, is presented by those around Vernon as entertainment. News crews swarm the town of Martirio after the shootings to capture the story of the shootings for viewers around the world. At the end of the book, death-row inmates are put on camera as entertainment, and television audiences are asked to decide whom should be executed next. Even the executions themselves are televised.

## *Sacrifice and Martyrdom*

Throughout the first part of the novel, Vernon

repeatedly remarks that the people around him are preparing to nail him to the cross, a reference to the crucifixion of Christ. In this way, Vernon suggests that he is being sacrificed for the sins of those around him, even though he himself has done nothing wrong. Later, Vernon sees the Spanish phrase "*Me ves, y sufres*" on the back of a truck in which he travels in Mexico; some believe that Jesus Christ spoke the words, which mean "see me, and suffer," as he was crucified. He ultimately tattoos the words across his chest in preparation for his execution.

Further, by naming Vernon's friend Jesus, the author draws a connection between Vernon's persecuted friend and Christ; Jesus Navarro, who is picked on by other students and sexually abused by his therapist, in a sense dies because of the sins of others. The author even uses the word "martirio"—Spanish for "martyrdom"—as the name of Vernon and Jesus's Texas hometown.

# *Fame*

In *Vernon God Little*, many of the characters act the way they do because they believe they have a chance to achieve fame after the tragedy at Martirio High School. This quest for fame is best embodied by Eulalio "Lally" Ledesma, who positions himself within the Little family by seducing Vernon's mother, only so he can set Vernon up as a villain for Lally's self-made news reports. Lally achieves the fame he seeks at the expense of Vernon's reputation and Doris's heart. He then promises the same fame to others, including the object of Vernon's affection, Taylor Figueroa, provided they help him come up with new stories that further cement Vernon's guilt and therefore increase Lally's own fame. Taylor Figueroa readily betrays Vernon's trust in her for a chance at stardom, and Doris's "friend" Leona just as eagerly steals away Lally for her shot at becoming a news anchor.

By contrast, fame for Vernon is a curse throughout the novel. It prevents him from maintaining his privacy, and after he runs away it limits his ability to travel unnoticed. Because of his fame—and the suggestibility of those who have seen him on the news—he is identified by witnesses to sixteen additional murders after the Martirio school shooting. In the end, Vernon is saved by his original attorney, Abdini, who is one of the few characters who does not seem to seek fame.

# Style

## *First-Person Narrative*

*Vernon God Little* uses a point of view known as first-person narrative. In a first-person narrative, one of the characters tells the story in his or her own words. A first-person narrative can be identified by the use of personal pronouns such as "I" and "me." In a first-person narrative, the reader learns the thoughts and feelings of the viewpoint character, though the thoughts and feelings of other characters remain unknown. In *Vernon God Little*, the story is told from the point of view of Vernon Gregory Little, who is also the main character. He tells the story in his own words, which creates a unique style and voice that reflects both his age and his attitude toward the world around him.

# Topics for Further Study

- In *Vernon God Little*, the last two chapters of the novel are open to interpretation by the reader. Some believe that the entire sequence after Vernon is strapped to the gurney exists only in Vernon's imagination. Some believe that the events actually occur, and offer a satisfying conclusion to the events of the book. What do you think? Write an essay explaining your opinion; be sure to include examples from the text that support your position.

- Throughout *Vernon God Little*, the narrator substitutes many other words that start with the letter "g" for his actual middle name, which is "Gregory." In the first chapter, for example, he refers to himself as "Vernon Genius Little." Take note of the many nicknames he gives himself throughout the book, and write a report listing the names and their significance to the character of Vernon. What do the names reveal about him? Why do you think the author uses "Vernon God Little" as the title of the book?

- The theme of cause and effect appears many times throughout

*Vernon God Little*. For example, when Vaine Gurie first questions Vernon in the police station, she gives him a speech about cause and effect; when Vernon is waiting on death row, he plays with a clacker-ball toy that demonstrates cause and effect. Write a report describing the theme of cause and effect as it appears throughout the novel, and explain how the idea of cause and effect influences Vernon's actions and attitudes.

- Throughout *Vernon God Little*, Vernon and the other characters frequently substitute incorrect sound-alike words for real words. Vernon says his dog is not a "rat-wheeler" instead of "rotweiller," and the courtroom typist is a "stainographer." Do these repeated misuses suggest anything about the characters in the novel? Write a paper identifying some of these mistakes, and explain whether you feel they enhance or detract from the authenticity of the novel's world.

- In small groups, brainstorm about how life would be if television viewers really could call and vote on events in the lives of private citizens. Outline a story—a farce, a cautionary tale, or any genre you like—that explores such a premise. Discuss the different ideas in a group.

## *Present Tense*

*Vernon God Little* is written in the present tense. This means that events are described as they are happening. Most contemporary stories are written in the past tense, telling what characters already did instead of what they currently do. Pierre's use of the present tense creates a sense of immediacy and urgency in the story, and, because the author never specifies a year in which the novel takes place, also suggests that the story might be happening right now.

## *Five-Act Structure*

The five-act structure is a type of story structure seen in many modern stories and plays; it is sometimes known as "Freytag's Pyramid," named for the German novelist and dramatist Gustav Freytag, who first described it after studying the works of William Shakespeare and the ancient Greeks. In a five-act structure, the first act generally presents exposition, or an explanation of the characters and the situations in which they find themselves. The second act consists of rising action, where the main character faces greater complications or obstacles to his or her goal. The third act consists of the climax or turning point, where the main character generally experiences a sudden change in fortune for better or worse. The fourth act contains the falling action; in this act, events play out as a result of the climax. The final act is known as the denouement, where the main conflict of the story is resolved.

Though the five-act structure is sometimes applied to stories and novels, these types of literary works are not usually broken down into acts as in a stage play. However, *Vernon God Little* is divided into five sections called "acts," much like a play would be. This emphasizes the notion that Vernon's story is being used by those around him to craft a sort of real-life television drama, and that nothing in his world is quite real.

## Historical Context

# *The Columbine High School Shootings*

On April 20, 1999, two students at Columbine High School near Littleton, Colorado, went on a shooting spree that resulted in the deaths of twelve students and one teacher, and the injury of two dozen others, before taking their own lives. It is the most infamous school shooting in American history.

The two Columbine shooters—Eric Harris and Dylan Klebold—were both seniors at the time and by all appearances planned the shooting far in advance. As early as 1997, Harris was posting death threats against other students on a website he created, as well as pictures and information about his experimentations with creating homemade bombs. Over a year before the shootings, the two were arrested for stealing computer equipment out of a parked van, but they avoided serious punishment by agreeing to participate in both counseling and community service programs. At around this time, the two began to accumulate an arsenal of weapons through friends and acquaintances, some of whom were later jailed for helping the two boys obtain guns illegally. Harris and Klebold also kept journals that suggested they were planning a large-scale bombing similar to the bombing in Oklahoma City in 1995, and they also wrote "hit lists" of students they wished to kill (though only one of their eventual victims was on such a list). Their original plan had been to blow up the Columbine High School cafeteria with two propane-based bombs that would detonate during the first lunch rush of the day. Afterward, they had planned to walk through the wreckage and shoot any remaining survivors.

On April 20, 1999, Harris and Klebold arrived at school just prior to the first lunch period and placed their two homemade bombs in the cafeteria. When the bombs failed to fully detonate, the two decided to open fire on students sitting on a grassy area outside the cafeteria. They soon made their way inside the school and to the library, where they shot and killed several more students and, from the library windows, attempted to shoot students as they were being evacuated from the rest of the building by police. Harris and Klebold spared several students, though their reasons for sparing these students are unknown. They left the library and went to other parts of the school, including the evacuated cafeteria, before returning to the library and taking their own lives. From start to finish, their rampage lasted less than an hour.

In the aftermath of the killings, there were several reports of a third shooter who had helped Harris and Klebold carry out the massacre. Police arrested a friend of the boys named Chris Morris on the day of the shootings, but he was later released. Another friend of the two, Nathan Dykeman, was also investigated as a possible accomplice, though witnesses confirmed that he was not at the school at the time of the shootings.

In *Vernon God Little*, Jesus Navarro kills sixteen in his school shooting spree—three more than in Columbine. Also, as with the Columbine shootings, Jesus's friend is almost immediately suspected of being an accomplice to the murders. When Vernon cannot prove his alibi, he is convicted and sentenced to death.

# Critical Overview

When *Vernon God Little* was first published in 2003, it received a wide range of critical responses. Some praised the novel, while others saw it as nothing more than an unfunny and uneven effort by a fledgling writer. This critical split decision even led to speculation that American reviewers were incapable of seeing the humor in a book that offers such a scathing critique of their own society.

In the *Guardian*, one of Britain's premier newspapers, Carrie O'Grady described the novel as "a startling and excellent debut." O'Grady also called the character of Vernon as "a brilliant comic creation." Joanne Wilkinson, in a review for *Booklist*, describes the book as "scatological, irreverent, crass, and very, very funny," and asserted that "Pierre is a comic anarchist with talent to spare." According to Wilkinson, "Every page is saturated with a humor that barely masks Pierre's contempt for the media, the criminal justice system, and the rampant materialism of contemporary culture."

Sam Sifton, writing for the *New York Times Book Review*, described *Vernon God Little* as "a dangerous, smart, ridiculous and very funny first novel." Sifton also called the book "a howl of satirical protest against much that helps define American culture to the rest of the world: reality television, fast food, religion, the death penalty."

Sifton felt Pierre's writing is "simply terrific" and noted that the author "renders adolescence brilliantly, capturing with seeming effortlessness the bright, contradictory hormone rush of teenage life." Sifton described the character of Vernon as "a deceptively simple boy who narrates this tale in the manner of a character created by Mark Twain and remixed by Dr. Dre."

Author Joyce Carol Oates echoed many of these sentiments in a review for the *New Yorker*. Oates wrote that the novel is "unexpectedly moving" and "raucous and brooding, coarse and lyric, corrosive and sentimental in about equal measure." Oates also noted that "Pierre has a flawless ear for adolescent-boy speech." However, Oates did concede that "the objects of Pierre's contempt—tabloid TV, consumer-culture idiocy, the American obsession with the sufferings of others, material goods, and 'image'—are not very original."

Other reviewers were not so kind. As an unnamed reviewer in *Kirkus Reviews* wrote, "Humor and mass murder make for strange bedfellows, and first-timer Pierre fails to find the tone that might harmonize them." The same reviewer argued that "there is no vision of [Vernon's] world," and that the book's "delayed revelation" about Jesus and the school shootings "is pointless and without suspense." In a review for *Publishers Weekly*, an unnamed critic stated:

> Most of the plotting feels like an excuse for Vernon's endless, sharply

snide riffs on his small town and the unique excesses of America that helped spawn the killings.... Vernon's voice grows tiresome, his excesses make him rather unlikable and the over-the-top, gross-out humor is hit-or-miss.

John Freeman, writing for the *Seattle Times*, also commented on the unlikable characters: "Not one character in these pages, including, eventually, Vernon God Little, earns our sympathy. They are uniformly cruel and crass to one another." Freeman also pointed out that the book "twists itself into a pretzel of unbelievable plotting and gross generalization" to convey its message.

Andrea Kempf, in a review for *Library Journal*, wrote of the novel, "The stereotypes are broad: poor Mexicans are noble; white Texans are idiots; women are mindless, materialistic gossips; and convicted murderers are more humane than people outside." Kempf also believed, "America may have difficulty finding the humor in this novel, but equally troubling is the inauthenticity of the narrative voice." Michiko Kakutani, in a review of the book for the *New York Times*, stated that "for the most part it is a lumbering, mannered performance, a vigorous but unimaginative compendium of every cliché you've ever heard about America in general and Texas in particular." Kakutani asserted that the author "fails to use the sort of telling details or surreal developments that might lend his story an eerie verisimilitude, or jolt the reader into a recognition of a larger truth." Kakutani concluded:

> In trying to score a lot of obvious points off a lot of obvious targets, Mr. Pierre may have won the Booker Prize and ratified some ugly stereotypes of Americans, but he hasn't written a terribly convincing or compelling novel.

*Vernon God Little* went on to win the 2003 Man Booker Prize, which is awarded to the best novel written by a citizen of the British Commonwealth or Ireland. The book also won the 2003 Whitbread Award for Best First Novel. Although some speculated that the book was poorly received by American critics because of its strong criticisms of American society, the reviews quoted here show that many American critics—including those for the *New Yorker* and the *New York Times Book Review*—actually praised the novel. The novel was also listed as a *New York Times* Notable Book for 2003.

# What Do I Read Next?

- *Hey Nostradamus!* is author Douglas Coupland's 2003 novel that revolves around a Columbine-like high school shooting. Coupland's massacre takes place in 1988 Vancouver, and in a unique twist, the story is narrated in part by one of the victims of the shooters.

- *Ludmila's Broken English* is DBC Pierre's second novel, published in 2006. The book intertwines the story of two once-conjoined British twins who have been separated from each other with the story of a young Russian woman desperate to find a way to support her family after she kills her incestuous grandfather. The two ultimately collide, thanks to an online scam for buying Russian brides.

- *Ultimate Punishment: A Lawyer's Reflections on Dealing with the Death Penalty* is lawyer-turned-author Scott Turow's 2004 nonfiction treatise on a subject with which he is intimately familiar, having served as both a prosecutor and an advocate for death-row inmates during his storied career. The book provides an objective and evenhanded look at both sides of the debate over capital punishment.

- Though written in the 1960s, John Kennedy Toole's comic novel *A Confederacy of Dunces* was first published in 1980—eleven years after the author killed himself. Toole was subsequently awarded a posthumous Pulitzer Prize for the novel, which chronicles the misadventures of eccentric New Orleans resident Ignatius J. Reilly as he embarks on a somewhat belated journey to start his working life in the French Quarter. Some critics have compared the absurd Texas of Pierre's *Vernon God Little* to Toole's quirky vision of New Orleans.

## Sources

Brockes, Emma, "How Did I Get Here? (interview with DBC Pierre)," in the *Guardian* (U.K.), October 16, 2003, books.guardian.co.uk/bookerprize2003/story/0,1063 (July 28, 2006).

Freeman, John, "'Huck Finn' Meets 'south Park' in 'Vernon God Little,'" in the *Seattle Times*, October 31, 2003, archives.seattletimes.nwsource.com (July 28, 2006).

Kakutani, Michiko, "Books of the Times; Deep in the Heart of Texas (via Australia)," in the *New York Times*, November 5, 2003, query.nytimes.com (July 28, 2006).

Kempf, Andrea, Review of *Vernon God Little*, in the *Library Journal*, Vol. 128, No. 16, October 1, 2003, p. 118.

Oates, Joyce Carol, "Showtime (review of *Vernon God Little*)," in the *New Yorker*, Vol. 79, Issue 32, October 27, 2003, p. 104.

O'Grady, Carrie, "Lone Star: Carrie O'Grady on DBC Pierre's Sparkling Debut, *Vernon God Little*," in *The Guardian*, January 18, 2003, books.guardian.co.uk/bookerprize2003/story/0,1019 (July 28, 2006).

Pierre, DBC, *Vernon God Little*, Harvest Books, 2004.

———, "Author's Statement," in *Contemporary Writers*, www.contemporarywriters.com/authors/?p=authD4F18F621669b19650jQlH252C46 (July 28, 2006).

Rees, Jasper, "Dirty Comes Clean," in *Telegraph.co.uk*, February 21, 2006, www.telegraph.co.uk (August 4, 2006).

"Report: Twelve Killed at Columbine in First Sixteen Minutes," in *CNN.com*, May 16, 2000, archives.cnn.com/2000/US/05/15/columbine.report.( (July 28, 2006).

Review of *Vernon God Little*, in *Kirkus Reviews*, Vol. 71, No. 15, August 1, 2003, p. 987.

Review of *Vernon God Little*, in *Publishers Weekly*, Vol. 250, No. 34, August 25, 2003, p. 39.

Sifton, Sam, "Holden Caulfield on Ritalin (Review of *Vernon God Little*)," in the *New York Times Book Review*, Vol. 108, November 9, 2003, p. 7, col. 1.

Wilkinson, Joanne, Review of *Vernon God Little*, in *Booklist*, Vol. 100, No. 1, September 1, 2003, p. 60.

# Further Reading

Brown, Brooks, and Rob Merritt, *No Easy Answers: The Truth Behind Death at Columbine*, Lantern Books, 2002.

> As a former friend of the two killers at Columbine, Brooks Brown—the boy who was famously warned by Eric Harris to leave the school grounds before the shooting started—was, like Vernon Little, suspected as an accomplice immediately after the shootings. In this book, he tells of his rocky relationship with the shooters, as well as the environment of persecution and bullying in which the murderers lived.

Radford, Benjamin, *Media Mythmakers: How Journalists, Activists and Advertisers Mislead Us*, Prometheus Books, 2003.

> In this book, Radford points out many examples of how different members of the media operate to serve their own needs above those of the public they purport to work for.

Salinger, J. D., *The Catcher in the Rye*, Little, Brown, 1991 (originally published in 1951).

> Many reviewers have compared Vernon Little to Holden Caulfield,

> the main character of this groundbreaking Salinger novel. Told from the point of view of Caulfield, *The Catcher in the Rye* set the groundwork for all future coming-of-age novels, including *Vernon God Little*.

Twain, Mark, *The Adventures of Huckleberry Finn*, Penguin Classics, 2002 (originally published in 1884).

> Considered by many to be the "Great American Novel," Twain's classic tale of one misfit boy's coming of age is still a shining example of unique narrative voice in American fiction. From its first line to its last, Finn's narrative is both authentic and revealing of his character.